ANCIENT CIVILIZATIONS

ANCIENT GREECE

D1708187

BY SARA GREEN

BELLWETHER MEDIA   MINNEAPOLIS, MN

Blastoff! Discovery launches a new mission: reading to learn. Filled with facts and features, each book offers you an exciting new world to explore!

This edition first published in 2020 by Bellwether Media, Inc.

No part of this publication may be reproduced in whole or in part without written permission of the publisher.
For information regarding permission, write to Bellwether Media, Inc.,
Attention: Permissions Department,
6012 Blue Circle Drive, Minnetonka, MN 55343.

Library of Congress Cataloging-in-Publication Data

Names: Green, Sara, 1964- author.
Title: Ancient Greece / By Sara Green.
Description: Minneapolis, MN : Bellwether Media, Inc., 2020. |
Series: Blastoff! Discovery: Ancient civilizations |
   Includes bibliographical references and index. |
Audience: Ages 7-13 | Audience: Grades 4-6 |
   Summary: "Engaging images accompany information about ancient
   Greece. The combination of high-interest subject matter and
   narrative text is intended for students in grades 3 through 8"–
   Provided by publisher.
Identifiers: LCCN 2019036010 (print) | LCCN 2019036011 (ebook) |
   ISBN 9781644871768 (library binding) | ISBN 9781618918604
   (paperback) | ISBN 9781618918529 (ebook)
Subjects: LCSH: Greece–Civilization–Juvenile literature. |
   Greece–History–Juvenile literature. | Greece–Social life and
   customs–Juvenile literature.
Classification: LCC DF741 .G736 2020 (print) | LCC DF741 (ebook) |
   DDC 938–dc23
LC record available at https://lccn.loc.gov/2019036010
LC ebook record available at https://lccn.loc.gov/2019036011

Editor: Kate Moening   Designer: Jeffrey Kollock

Printed in the United States of America, North Mankato, MN.

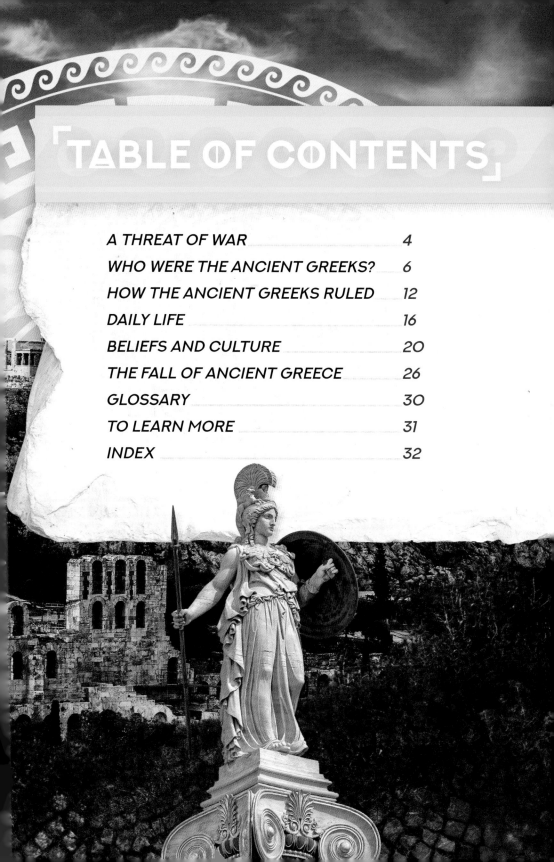

TABLE OF CONTENTS

A THREAT OF WAR

MODERN-DAY ATHENS

The sun blazes over the Greek **city-state** of Athens. A boy dashes home from school. He has heard rumors of war with another city-state called Sparta.

GROUP OF HOPLITES

The boy finds his mother in the courtyard making dinner. He shares his worries about Sparta. Its army is the fiercest in the land. The boy's father will have to serve as a **hoplite**. Can Athens survive this war?

WHO WERE THE ANCIENT GREEKS?

ANCIENT GREECE IN
THE CLASSICAL PERIOD

Greek territory

BLACK
SEA

ADRIATIC
SEA

AEGEAN
SEA

IONIAN
SEA

MEDITERRANEA
SEA

N
W E
S

Ancient Greece was a civilization from around 1200 BCE to 31 BCE. At its largest, it covered all of modern-day Greece and the western coast of Turkey. It also included many islands in the Mediterranean, Aegean, and Ionian Seas. Because of its location, ancient Greeks were skilled sailors. This boosted trade to help Greece grow.

The Greeks called themselves *Hellenes*. The name came from a character in Greek **mythology**. Ancient Greece reached its height of **culture** during its **Classical Period**. During this time, Greece may have numbered more than 2 million people.

PERIODS OF ANCIENT GREECE

GREEK DARK AGES	around 1200 – 800 BCE
ARCHAIC PERIOD	around 800 – 480 BCE
CLASSICAL PERIOD	around 480 – 323 BCE
HELLENISTIC AGE	323 BCE – 31 BCE

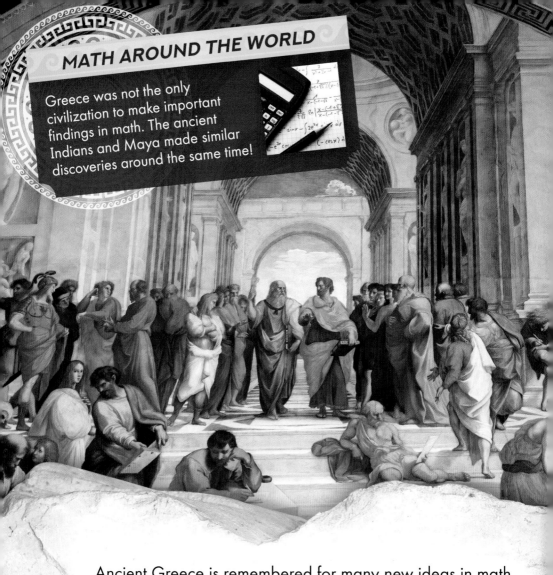

MATH AROUND THE WORLD

Greece was not the only civilization to make important findings in math. The ancient Indians and Maya made similar discoveries around the same time!

Ancient Greece is remembered for many new ideas in math, art, government, and **philosophy**. Greeks even created the first Olympic Games! Athens founded the first **democracy**. The city-state became the Greek center for learning and knowledge.

Greek philosophers changed the way people thought. Many of their ideas are still used today! Plato and Aristotle were among the first to understand the world through **logic**. Plato's teacher, Socrates, did not give students answers. Instead, he asked questions to have students think for themselves.

ARISTOTLE

WHO WAS ARISTOTLE?   philosopher in ancient Greece

WHEN DID HE LIVE?   around 384 to 322 BCE

WHERE DID HE LIVE?   Athens

WHY IS HE IMPORTANT?

- changed the way philosophers thought about morals
- introduced scientific observation that scientists still use today
- his ideas about logic are still taught today

WHAT IS HE KNOWN FOR?

- invented the field of logic
- became the first European thinker to study science through observation
- founded the first research school in Europe

9

Ancient Greeks did not think of Greece as one country. Instead, the region was divided into independent communities called city-states. Mountains, seas, and a rocky landscape made travel difficult. They kept city-states separated.

Greece eventually had more than 1,000 city-states. Each had its own rulers, laws, and customs. But city-states also had things in common. They shared the same language and gods. Many religious sites were shared. Over time, city-states shared the same alphabet, too.

ON THE MAP

The Greek term for city-state was *polis*. This word is still used in city names today. Minneapolis, Annapolis, and Indianapolis all come from Greek!

DELPHI, GREECE, A SHARED RELIGIOUS SITE

THINK ABOUT IT

What makes city-states different from cities?

HOW THE ANCIENT GREEKS RULED

PERIANDER, THE
TYRANT OF CORINTH

Most Greek city-states, including Sparta, were oligarchies. In other places, such as Corinth, tyrants took control by force. A handful of regions had monarchies.

In 510 BCE, Athenians **revolted** against their tyrant leader. By 508, the city-state had created a democracy. It allowed all free adult men to vote. The democracy lasted nearly 200 years. Then King Philip II of Macedonia took control and returned Athens to a single ruler.

DEMOCRACY

Democracy produced some of Greece's most important thinkers and helped Athens flourish. This government system forever changed world history!

HOW DEMOCRACY HELPED ATHENS GROW

- ☑ helped poor people to vote by paying them
- ☑ created a more equal society
- ☑ brought more stability to Athens through equality
- ☑ grew trade through new ideas and different voices
- ☑ brought together wisdom and skills of citizens from all areas
- ☑ gave people more opportunities to learn, invent, and make art through equality

THINK ABOUT IT

How could the decades of fighting in the Peloponnesian War have weakened both Sparta and Athens?

War helped ancient Greek city-states expand and control their borders. During the Persian Wars from 492 to 449 BCE, city-states fought together. They defeated the powerful Persian Empire.

At other times, city-states fought against each other. From 431 to 404 BCE, Athens and Sparta battled for territory in the bloody Peloponnesian War. Sparta won, but years of fighting weakened both sides. In 338 BCE, Philip II conquered Greece. His son, Alexander the Great, divided up the region. Alexander brought Greek culture to many other parts of his empire.

ALEXANDER THE GREAT

FARMLAND IN GREECE

Most Greeks were farmers. Men with the best farmland were often the wealthiest and most powerful. Men also worked as soldiers and traders. The least powerful Greeks were laborers, slaves, and women.

In most city-states, women rarely left the house except to attend religious ceremonies and public baths. Instead, they worked inside the home and cared for children. They cooked outside in small courtyards. Only the largest homes had indoor kitchens and baths.

CLASSICAL PERIOD
ATHENS AND SPARTA

ACHIEVEMENTS
lasting additions to the arts, philosophy, science

GOVERNMENT
democracy: citizens vote to make decisions

ATHENS

POPULATION
40,000 citizens;
40,000 slaves;
80,000 others

LIFESTYLE
luxuries and food from all over, with fine houses for the wealthy

EDUCATION
boys: math, reading, writing, some military
girls: spinning, weaving

FOCUS
trade

ACHIEVEMENTS
fearsome military power

GOVERNMENT
oligarchy: two kings make all decisions

SPARTA

POPULATION
8,000 citizens;
100,000 slaves

LIFESTYLE
simple food, with men living in military housing

EDUCATION
boys: military focus, some reading and writing
girls: athletics focus, some reading and writing

FOCUS
military

SPARTAN AGOGE

   In most Greek city-states, only boys attended school.
They learned math, reading, and writing. Many learned to play
a musical instrument. Mothers taught their daughters at home.
Girls learned to cook, weave, and take care of the household.

   Sparta was different. From ages 7 to 20, Spartan boys attended
schools called *agoges*. They learned military skills and self-control
to be good citizens. Adult men committed their lives to the army.
Spartan girls also went to school. They learned athletic skills.
Only wealthy Spartans learned to read.

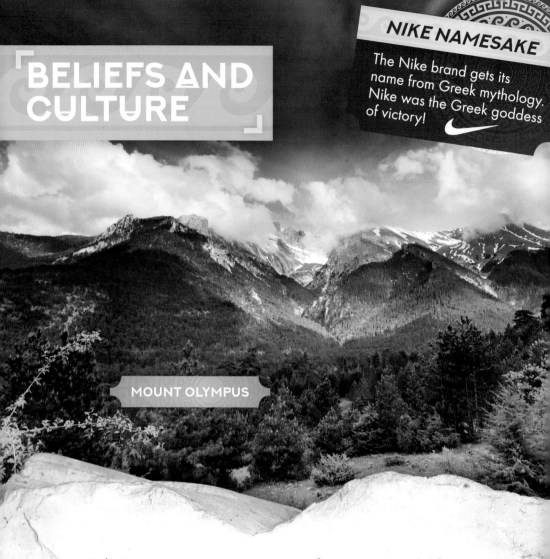

BELIEFS AND CULTURE

MOUNT OLYMPUS

Religion was an important part of ancient Greek life. The Greeks believed in dozens of gods and goddesses. The twelve most important were a family who lived on Mount Olympus. Each god controlled a different part of life, such as the weather or the environment. Priests were both men and women who served specific gods.

Myths about the gods guided Greek values and actions. Greeks often looked for signs from the gods to tell the future. They thanked the gods with food, flowers, and other offerings.

GREEK GODS AND GODESSES

HADES
- god of the underworld
- Zeus's brother

POSEIDON
- god of the sea, earthquakes, storms, and horses
- Zeus's brother

ZEUS
- god of the sky and thunder
- king of the gods
- controlled the weather

HERA
- goddess of women, family, and marriage
- Zeus's wife and queen of the gods

ATHENA
- goddess of wisdom, skill, and war
- Zeus's daughter

APOLLO
- god of music, arts, crops, and herds
- Zeus's son

Religion often inspired Greek art. Many temples honored the gods and goddesses. The most famous of these is called the Parthenon. It was built for Athena. The Parthenon overlooks Athens from a hill called the Acropolis.

PARTHENON, GREECE

The gods also appeared in Greek pottery and sculpture. Artists painted scenes of gods and myths. They sculpted smooth marble statues of the gods. The Greeks valued simplicity, beauty, and order. Art and **architecture** reflected these ideals.

THINK ABOUT IT

Athena was the goddess of wisdom and war. Why would the people of Athens build their most famous temple for her? Why would they put the temple on a hill above the city?

Storytelling was another important part of Greek life. Epic poems such as the *Iliad* and the *Odyssey* were first passed down orally. But during the 8th century BCE, the Greek alphabet was developed. A poet named Homer wrote the poems down. Many students still read them today!

GREEK IN ENGLISH

Greek uses a different alphabet. But it can be written with the English alphabet so we can read it!

ENGLISH	GREEK	MEANING
alphabet	alpha + beta	alpha and beta are the first two letters of the Greek alphabet
dinosaur	deinos + savra	terrible + lizard
music	muses	the Muses were goddesses of arts and sciences
planets	planomai	to wander, wandering stars
telephone	tele + phōn	far + sound

A POWERFUL LANGUAGE

The Greeks changed literature and language far beyond Greece. English has more than 150,000 words that come from Greek!

Ω

The new writing system led to even more Greek literature. Historians recorded important wars and events. Philosophy books explained how to live a good life. Plays taught people about history, moral lessons, or myths!

THE FALL OF ANCIENT GREECE

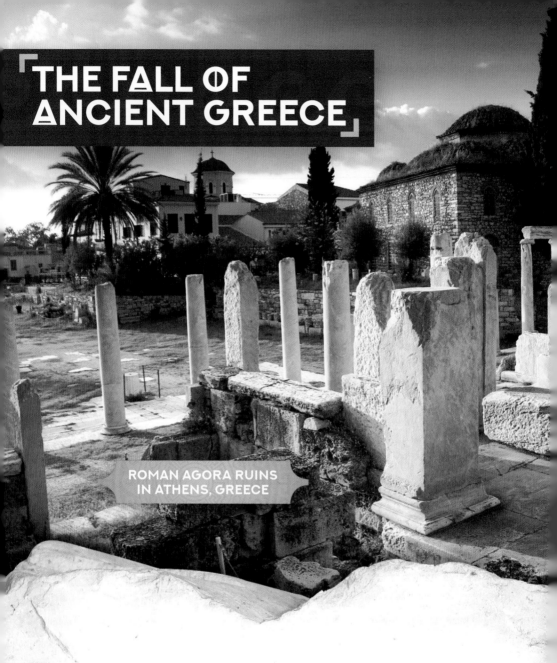

ROMAN AGORA RUINS IN ATHENS, GREECE

Ancient Greece controlled the Mediterranean region for centuries. Alexander the Great spread Greek culture throughout the Macedonian empire. But the empire fell apart when Alexander died in 323 BCE. Warfare became common between Greece and other former Macedonian states.

Meanwhile, Rome was gaining power. In 146 BCE, the Romans seized mainland Greece. But they did not destroy Greece completely. Romans respected and even copied Greek philosophy, religion, and architecture. In 31 BCE, Rome officially brought Greece under Roman rule. The great city-states would never return.

ANCIENT GREEK TIMELINE

508 BCE
democracy begins in Athens

480 BCE
Greek Classical Period begins

31 BCE
Greece becomes officially ruled by the Roman Empire

800–700 BCE
Greek alphabet is invented

338 BCE
Phillip II of Macedonia takes control of Greece

146 BCE
Rome seizes and claims control of Greece

Today, Greece is a small country of nearly 11 million people. Many ancient ruins stand among newer buildings. Sites like the Parthenon offer important clues about the ancient world.

Ancient Greek culture continues to impact **Western civilization**. Modern buildings feature ancient Greek columns. Many students learn through teaching methods from ancient philosophers. Democracy is now an important form of government across the globe. Ancient Greece has long passed, but its culture still inspires people today!

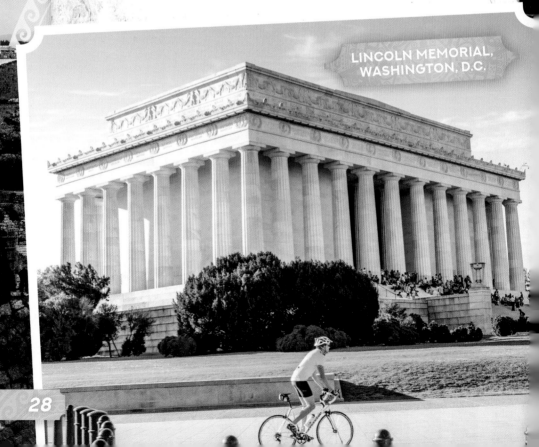

LINCOLN MEMORIAL, WASHINGTON, D.C.

MODERN-DAY ATHENS

GLOSSARY

architecture—the design of buildings and other structures

city-state—a self-governing city and its surrounding area

Classical Period—a time in ancient Greece when the civilization reached new heights in culture, art, and ideas; the Classical Period happened around 480 to 323 BCE.

culture—the specific beliefs and practices of a group or region

democracy—a government that allows people to vote and have a say in how the government is run

hoplite—a heavily armed foot soldier of ancient Greece

logic—a way of thinking that uses careful reasoning and evidence to explain events; before logic developed, most people understood the world through mythology.

monarchies—forms of government with one ruler; rule of monarchies is often passed down through familes.

mythology—the ideas or stories of a particular group or culture; mythology usually includes beings with superhuman powers.

oligarchies—governments run by a few wealthy people

philosophy—the study of ideas about knowledge, thinking, and the meaning of life

revolted—violently fought the rule of a leader or government

tyrants—people who rule with absolute power

Western civilization—the modern culture of North America and western Europe

AT THE LIBRARY

Cottrell, George. *Ancient Greece*. New York, N.Y.: KidHaven Publishing, 2017.

Hudak, Heather C. *Forensic Investigations of the Ancient Greeks*. New York, N.Y.: Crabtree Publishing Company, 2019.

Randolph, Joanne. *The Myths and Legends of Ancient Greece and Rome*. New York, N.Y.: Cavendish Square Publishing, 2018.

ON THE WEB

FACTSURFER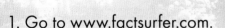

Factsurfer.com gives you a safe, fun way to find more information.

1. Go to www.factsurfer.com.

2. Enter "ancient Greece" into the search box and click 🔍.

3. Select your book cover to see a list of related web sites.

INDEX

The images in this book are reproduced through the courtesy of: Andrew Mayovskyy, cover; Dimitrios, p. 3; S. Borisov, pp. 4-5; Lanmas/ Alamy, pp. 5, 21 (Hades); spiber.de, p. 8 (fun fact); Viacheslav Lopatin, pp. 8, 22-23; Julian Popov, p. 9; Oleg Atlantic, p. 9 (landscape); Jingwen Yao, p. 10; Mapics, pp. 10-11; Paulus Moreelse, p. 12; Georgios Kollidas, p. 13; Tatiana Popova, p. 13 (landscape); North Wind Picture Archives/ Alamy, pp. 14-15, 17 (top), 19; Placido Costanzi, p. 15; Alex Ionas, pp. 16-17; image collection by Bildagentur-online/ Alamy, p. 17 (left); Patryk Kosmider, p. 17 (right); WitR, p. 18; Lev Paraskevopoulos, p. 20; Stig Alenas p. 21 (Poseidon); IMG Stock Studio, p. 21 (Zeus); Gilmanshin, p. 21 (Hera); NCKAHDEP, p. 21 (Athena); Kozlik, p. 21 (Apollo); Elena11, p. 24 (Jupiter); Freedom Life, p. 24 (guitar); Herschel Hoffmeyer, p. 24 (T. rex); Classic Image/ Alamy, p. 25; Inu, p. 26; Anton_Ivanov, p. 28; cge2010, pp. 28-29; Sergei Denisov, p. 30